TIMELESS
INDIA

TIMELESS INDIA

Ian Westwell

CHARTWELL
BOOKS, INC.

This edition published in 2007 by

CHARTWELL BOOKS, INC.
A Division of
BOOK SALES, INC.
114 Northfield Avenue
Edison, New Jersey 08837

ISBN-13: 978-0-7858-2317-9
ISBN-10: 0-7858-2317-4

© 2007 Compendium Publishing, 43 Frith Street,
London, Soho, W1V 4SA, United Kingdom

Cataloging-in-Publication data is available from the
Library of Congress

Printed and bound in China

Design: Compendium Design

PAGE 2: A challenging and slow trek is the only way to
get to see the beauty of Konze La Pass high up in
Ladakh at 3,076 feet above sea level.

PAGE 4: Building first started on Amber Fort in
Rajasthan in the 11th century but this massive and
highly impressive palace and fort complex was
continually improved and extended. See pages 70 to 75.

Contents

Introduction

Introduction

India covers a land area of around 1.25 million square miles, roughly 2.4 percent of the Earth's surface, but it is home to close to 17 percent of the world's population. As befits a country of this size and populousness, it is diverse in almost every respect.

Geographically the subcontinent can be divided into five distinctive regions. Beginning with the north, there are the Himalayas that are the world's highest and youngest mountain range and date back some 80 million years. Actually a series of ranges and valleys, they run roughly southeast to northwest and largely mark the country's northern borders. They contain the highest mountain in India, Khangchendzonga (28,208 feet) in West Bengal, and are actually growing at a rate of 0.03in per year. The most southerly range of the Himalayas gives way to the next import region—the great northern plain. This begins in the northwest of the country and runs eastward from Delhi to the Bay of Bengal, falling a mere 656 feet along the way. The plain also contains the headwaters of two of the region's greatest rivers—the Ganges, which drains most of the plain before uniting with the Brahmaputra to flow into the Bay of Bengal, and the Indus that largely flows through neighboring Pakistan before entering the Arabian Sea.

PREVIOUS PAGE: **High up in the Himalaya Mountains Gokyo Valley leads up to Everest Base Camp.**

RIGHT: **Qutub Minar is a 239 foot high sandstone tower of victory that stands in the Qutab Complex near Delhi. It was completed in three distinct stages starting in 1199 and finished in 1370.**

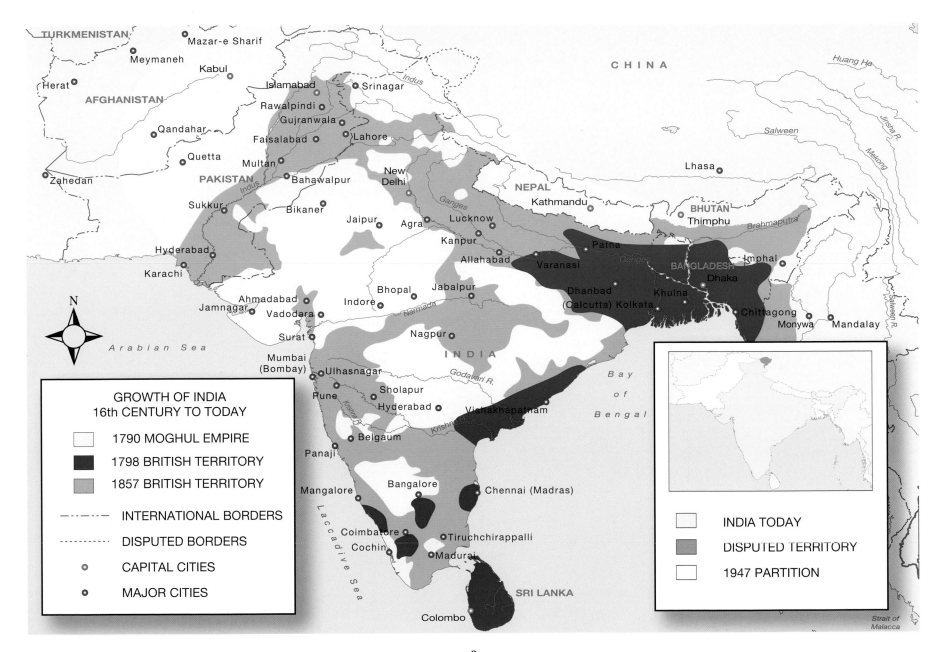

TURKMENISTAN
Mazar-e Sharif
Meymaneh
Kabul
Herat
AFGHANISTAN
Qandahar
Quetta
Zahedan
PAKISTAN
Islamabad
Rawalpindi
Gujranwala
Faisalabad
Multan
Bahawalpur
Srinagar
Lahore
Indus
Sukkur
Bikaner
Hyderabad
Karachi
Jaipur
Agra
New
Delhi
Ganges
Lucknow
Kanpur
Allahabad
Ahmadabad
Jamnagar
Vadodara
Indore
Bhopal
Jabalpur
Narmada
Surat
Nagpur
Mumbai
(Bombay)
Ulhasnagar
Sholapur
Pune
Hyderabad
Belgaum
Panaji
Godavari R.
Krishna
Mangalore
Bangalore
Coimbatore
Cochin
Tiruchchirappalli
Madurai
Laccadive
Sea
Arabian Sea
CHINA
Huang Ha
Salween
Jinsha R.
Mekong
Lhasa
NEPAL
Kathmandu
BHUTAN
Thimphu
Brahmaputra
Patna
Varanasi
Ganges
BANGLADESH
Imphal
Dhanbad
(Calcutta) Kolkata
Khulna
Dhaka
Chittagong
Monywa
Mandalay
Salween R.
INDIA
Bay
of
Bengal
Vishakhapatnam
Chennai (Madras)
SRI LANKA
Colombo
Strait of
Malacca

GROWTH OF INDIA
16th CENTURY TO TODAY

1790 MOGHUL EMPIRE
1798 BRITISH TERRITORY
1857 BRITISH TERRITORY
INTERNATIONAL BORDERS
DISPUTED BORDERS
CAPITAL CITIES
MAJOR CITIES

N

INDIA TODAY
DISPUTED TERRITORY
1947 PARTITION

The central and southern zones can be treated as one region. This begins south of the northern plain, where the land rises to what is known as the Deccan Plateau. This is bordered to the east and west by ranges of hills—the Ghats—that run approximately parallel to the respective coastlines. The Western Ghats, which are higher and have a wider coastal plain, also contain the headwaters of the region's two main rivers, the Godavari and the Krishna, both of which flow across the plateau to the east coast and then into the Bay of Bengal. The next region, the western region, divides India from Pakistan and consists of a number of distinctive areas. To the north lies Kashmir, part of the Himalayas, and this gives way to the Punjabi plains and the Great Thar desert that covers western Rajasthan. The next area lies in Gujarat and is the Rann of Kutch. This is a large area of seasonal marshland that is a mixture of water and isolated islands during the wet season (June–August) but little more than a flat plain in the dry season (November–April). Islands make up the final region. These, the Andaman and Nicobar Islands, comprise some 570 coral atolls on the eastern margin of the Bay of Bengal that stretch over 3,280 miles down the Bay of Bengal ending near the Indonesian island of Sumatra.

The people of India

India is currently the second most populous country on Earth and will probably overtake China in the next few decades to take the number one spot. The most recent ten-yearly census in 2001 revealed that India's population stood at 1,027,015,247, a figure showing a staggering increase of 21.34 percent over the 1991 return. There is a growing imbalance in the sexes; in 1991 there were 972 females for every 1,000 males but the former figure fell to 933 in 2001. The vast majority of people (75 percent) live in rural areas but some of the country's cities are of staggering (and growing) size—for Mumbai the figure is 16.37 million people and 13.22 million for Kolkata.

Thanks to a system of compulsory and free education until the age of 14, India had a literacy rate of around 65 percent in 2001 but this figure masks various disparities. Although official figures indicate that some two-thirds of eligible children are enroled in school, many, especially those in rural areas, do

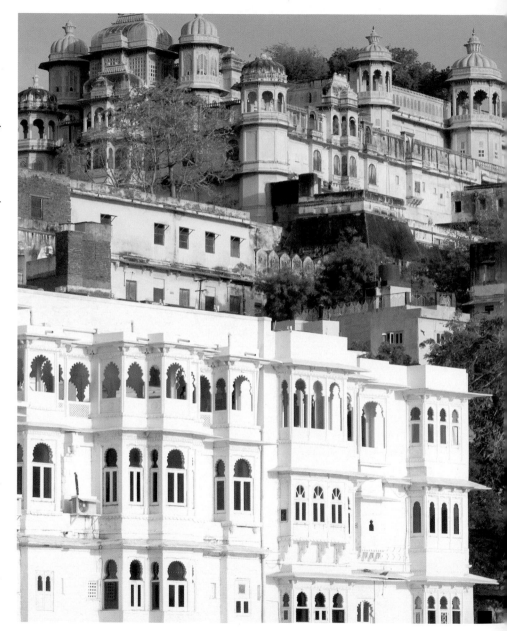

not attend regularly or drop out to work on the land before reaching the official leaving age. The figure of 65 percent is also somewhat misleading as it hides gender inequality; while the literacy rate for males stands as 76 percent, it is a much lower 54 percent for females.

India is also home to many languages. English, one of two official languages, is widely spoken, while Hindi, the other with official status, is the first tongue of 30 percent of the population. Bengali, Telugu and Marathi are each spoken by eight percent of the population, while other significant languages are Tamil (7 percent), Urdu (5 percent), and Gujarati (5 percent). There are also more than 1,500 recognized minor languages spoken across the sub-continent. Although India is largely homogeneous when its comes to religious affiliation with 82 percent practising Hinduism, it is also home to followers of Sunni Islam (11 percent) and Christianity (3 percent) as well as having devotees of Buddhism (7 million people), Jainism (4 million), Judaism (30,000), Sikhism (18 million), and Zoroastrianism (90,000).

Indian society is not only divided between rich and poor. Hinduism has also brought about the largely rigid caste system. It central tenet is that individuals are born into a certain caste (varna) and, if they lead a largely blameless life and fulfil their duty (dharma), they will be reborn into a higher caste. There are four castes—(Brahmin) priests, Kshatriya (warriors), Vaishya (merchants), and Sudra (peasants). Below these ranks are the so-called Dalits, individuals previously known as Untouchables but now officially referred to as Scheduled Castes who are responsible for the most menial and unpleasant tasks of all. There have been attempts to improve the lot of the Scheduled Castes, such as setting quotas for them in public sector jobs, seats in parliament, and places at university, but there has been some resistance to these efforts.

LEFT: The largest palace complex in Rajasthan is the City Palace in Udaipur, much of which now houses a magnificent museum. The palace is built from granite and marble and was originally built by Maharana Udai Singh of the Sisodia Rajput clan and then considerably extended and embellished by his descendants.

Government and the economy

India is a federal republic and constitutional democracy (enacted on January 26, 1950) in which anyone over the age of 18 can vote at state and national level. The country is split into 29 states and six union territories. The former have their own legislatures of various types with a governor appointed by the president who can assume wide powers in a state-wide emergency, while the latter are run by an administrator who is also appointed by the president. One controversial statute in the constitution—known as the President's Rule—allows the central government to take over the running of a state in the case of an emergency.

The national parliament comprises two chambers, the lower House of the People (Lok Sabha) and the upper Council of States (Rajya Sabha). The former has 545 representatives (including 125 seats reserved for members of the Scheduled Castes and Tribes) and elections have to take place every five years unless one is called by the ruling government in the interim. The Council of States has 245 members who are elected for terms of six years with a third standing for re-election every two years. Most of them are elected by state legislatures on a quota system although 12 seats are in the gift of the president. Presidents are elected by votes in both chambers every five years and are advised by a council of ministers that is appointed by the prime minister. Although presidents perform a largely ceremonial role, they do have the power to dissolve the lower but not the upper chamber.

The Indian economy

For the first 40 or so years after independence the economy was state planned but this policy was ended in 1991, not least because the country's share of

RIGHT: A ceremonial elephant painted and clothed for a festival.

FAR RIGHT: Hamida Banu Begum, Humayun's widow ordered the building of her husband Emperor Humayun's mausoleum. Building started in 1562 and took eight years. The architects were probably Sayyed Muhammad ibn Mirak Ghiyathuddin and his father Mirak Ghiyathuddin from Herat.

world trade had fallen from 2 percent in the 1950s to a mere 0.5 percent in the 1980s. The opening up of the economy had an almost immediate and profound impact on the country's fortunes; the role of the public sector in the national economy fell dramatically and there was a significant rise in inward investment from foreign businesses. Indian exports eventually skyrocketed while imports remained steady, producing an ongoing economic boom.

This boom is based on the roughly 7,500 different commodities that India exports to close on 200 countries. The United States is the biggest export market and earned the country nearly $18 billion in 2002. Agriculture is still the dominant sector of the economy—something like 65 percent of the labor force works on the land and they generate around 25 percent of the country's gross domestic product. The main crops are fruit and vegetables, milk, wheat, rice, sugar, tea, and rubber. Indian industry is made up of thousands of small-scale enterprises with a handful of major corporations. Textile manufacture remains the big player in the economy, generating roughly one third of its export earnings and employing a staggering 90 million or so people. However, in addition, the current boom is producing a wave of diversification, not least into information technology; the software sector only really began in the 1980s but by 2001 it accounted for 15 percent of Indian's exports.

Tourism is another key industry that is both a major employer (15.5 million people) and a significant earner of foreign currency. Around 2.65 million visitors traveled to India in 2000, roughly 0.4 percent of the world's total. This figure is likely to rise in the future if India invests in better transport facilities, develops better tourist-related infrastructure and adopts a more aggressive approach to marketing. India has an enormously rich and extremely diverse cultural history that is expressed through the various art forms such as literature, music, painting, and sculpture. Nevertheless, is perhaps architecture that best exemplifies the many peoples who have contributed to the culture of India and attracts travelers in their millions.

LEFT: One of the most beautiful, most recognizable, and most photographed building in the world, the Taj Mahal is recognized as a geniunely great work of art and architecture.

LEFT: View of the Taj Mahal from Musamman Burj, the large octagonal tower within the compund of Agra Fort. Shah Jahan was imprisoned in the tower for seven years after being deposed by his son Aurangzeb, but at least he could gaze upon the tomb of his beloved Mumtaz Mahal and ponder her extravagant mausoleum that virtually bankrupted his kingdom and lost him his throne. Local legend says that this is the last view enjoyed by Shah Jehan before he died.

ABOVE: Amber Fort near Jaipur in Rajasthan is one of the most imposing and impressive forts in India. It is a fortified palace complex started in 1592 by Raja Man Singh, commander in chief of Akbar's army and continuously improved by successive rulers for the following150 years. The town of Amber is dedicated to Amba, the Mother Goddess, also called Gatta Rani or Queen of the Pass.

LEFT: Mount Everest in the Himalaya range is the highest mountain on Earth above sea level and is visible from India although it is located on the border between between Nepal and China.

FAR LEFT: The Himalayas overlook Leh Palace (center left of photograph) which itself overlooks the town of Leh. The palace was built by King Sengge Namgyal in the 17th century who modeled it on the Potala Palace in Tibet. The nine storey palace was occupied by the royal family until the mid 19th century when they moved to Stok Palace in Ladakah as Kashmiri forces threatened to overwhelm them. Although a long time ruin the palace is currently being restored.

ABOVE: The Indian rhino has been brought back from the brink of extinction by strict protection laws. Despite the law, they are still targets for poachers.

RIGHT: The sacred Ganga river (Ganges) starts as meltwater from Gangotri Glacier in the Indian state of Uttaranchal and runs across India 1,557 miles to the Bay of Bengal.

LEFT: The small town of Jharkot is dwarfed by the colossal mountains around it, when the winter snows arrive the villagers are completely isolated from the rest of the world.

ABOVE: Ajanta Caves in Maharashtra contain some of the very earliest Buddhist paintings and carvings that date right back to the 2nd century B.C.

23

ABOVE: A precarious-seeming bridge across a remote gorge in Zanskar in Kargil district, which lies in the eastern half of the Indian state of Jammu and Kashmir.

RIGHT: The vast Himalaya range is the source of three of the world's major river systems—the Indus Basin, the Ganga-Brahmaputra Basin, and the Yangtze Basin.

Early Civilizations: 2500 B.C.–A.D. 510

Early Civilizations:
c.2500 B.C.–A.D. 510

The first civilization on the sub-continent to be identified by archaeologists is known as the Harappan culture, which flourished around 2500 B.C. in the Indus valley in what is now Pakistan but whose influence spread into India. The Harappans developed large cities such as Lothal in India, established religious practices, created a written language and traded as far afield as Mesopotamia (now Iraq). The culture declined in the second millennium B.C. but the exact cause remains a matter of scholarly debate—climate change, flooding, and invasions have all been suggested.

The rapid growth of Aryan influence in India from around 1500 B.C. is again a matter of discussion, although all agree they were responsible for

PAGE 26–27: Mahabalipuram is a town in Kancheepuram district in the Indian state of Tamil Nadu that during the 7th century was the most important port of the South Indian dynasty of the Pallavas. Here, between the 7th and 9th centuries, so many amazing historic monuments were built that the area has now become a UNESCO World Heritage Site. Most of the monuments, which include temples and cave temples, sculpted reliefs, and monolithic chariots known as *rathas*, are cut out of the rock and date to the early stages of Dravidian architecture.

RIGHT: The Ellora Caves are in Maharashtra, near the old caravan route linking the prosperous northern cities to the ports on the west coast of India. The caves date to 600 A.D. and a period when the similar but much older caves at Ajunta were abandoned; there are 34 caves of either Jain, Hindu, or Buddhist observance.

FAR RIGHT: Ellora cave 16 is carved from a lump of solid basalt as a recreation of Mount Kailash—Shiva and Parvati's Himalayan home and the axis between heaven and earth. The rock is the world's largest monolith and was originally coated with brilliant white lime plaster so as to resemble a snowy mountain.

Hinduism's sacred texts, the Vedas. Some suggest they were originally invaders or migrants into northwest India from Afghanistan and Central Asia; others believe that they were in fact the original inhabitants. Whichever the case the Aryans slowly coalesced into four great kingdoms and during the 5th century B.C. two, Kosala and Magadha, became pre-eminent. The latter became the most powerful when the Nanda dynasty assumed the throne in 364 B.C.

The next great empire emerged in 321 B.C., when Chandragupta Maurya seized the Magadha throne from the Nanda. He ruled from Pataliputra (Patna) and established a dynasty that saw the Maurya Empire spread across central, eastern, and western India. It reached its greatest extent under Ashoka but underwent a terminal decline after his death, finally disappearing in 184 B.C. India became the home of several smaller empires after the decline of the Mauryas—the Sungas, the Shakas, the Kushanas, and the Shatavahanas. Despite the lack of a guiding central authority and various rivalries, this was a time of expansion. Trade with Europe became well established, while both Buddhism and Jainism, which had emerged around 500 B.C., grew enormously in popularity even though both religions split along doctrinal lines.

Another major empire emerged in A.D. 319 when the king of the little-known Gupta tribe, Chandragupta I, married a royal daughter of the Licchavis, one of the most powerful groups in the north. Gupta power now expanded rapidly, not least under Chandragupta II. Wealth accrued so that money was showered on the arts, education, and religion. Although the Guptas were Buddhists, both it and Jainism began to decline in popularity in the face of a resurgent interest in Hinduism. The Gupta Empire flourished until the early 6th century but defeat at the hands of the invading nomadic Huns in 510 led to its demise. North India then broke up into various petty Hindu kingdoms and remained fragmented until the arrival of Muslim invaders in the 11th century.

RIGHT AND FAR RIGHT: Archaeological research shows that the caves at Ellora were occupied for around 500 years during which time their elaborate carvings and sculptures were made. Although damaged during the 13th century Muslim iconoclastic upsurge, the damage was minimal thanks to the exceptional hardness of the basalt rock from which they are cut.

RIGHT: In the state of Bihar is Bodhgaya, one of the four most important Buddhist pilgramage centers in the world as it was here that the Buddha attained supreme enlightenment while sitting under the Bodhi Tree. A tree grown from a cutting taken from the original Bodhi tree still grows on the temple premesis. Under the shade of this tree is the Vajrasan (or diamond throne), a large red sandstone rock on which the Buddha reputedly sat.

FAR RIGHT: The principal building at Bodhgaya is Mahabodi Temple that stands on the site of a shrine erected by Ashoka in the 3rd century B.C. The temple was restored in the 11th century, and then again in 1882, and is claimed to be an exact replica of the original 7th century temple. From the 48 square feet base the temple rises like a slender pyramid to a cylindrical top, 170 feet high. Inside the main chamber sits an enormous, 164 foot high, gilded Buddha cut from black stone.

LEFT: At Pattadakal in Karnataka, there are nine Hindu temples dating from the 7th and 8th centuries. They are covered with beautiful narrative sculptural reliefs depicting many of the great stories from the Hindu literature.

ABOVE: The temple complex at Madurai in Tamil Nadu is dominated by the Meenakshi Sundareswarar temple that attracts thousands of Hindu worshippers. According to legend, this is where Shiva and the fish-eyed goddess, Meenakshi, married.

LEFT: One of 24 stone-carved solar wheels from the Konarak Sun Temple near Puri. The wheels date from 1240 and are part of the medieval Orissan architecture that has made this location a UNESCO World Heritage Site.

FAR LEFT: Stone temple carvings at Konark, Orissa. The partially ruined temple is dedicated to Surya Devi, the Sun god and was originally built on the edge of the ocean, although that has now receded. The temple was built in the 13th century by King Narasimhadeva and was designed in the shape of a celestial chariot for transporting the Sun god, Surya, across the heavens. Seven horses pull his 24-wheeled chariot (there are 12 wheels on each side of the building). Each horse represents a day of the week with each wheel symbolizing a period of time.

LEFT: Kapaleeswarar Temple (Tirumayilai Shivastalam) is a modern recreation from descriptions of ancient Puranams and the Tevaram in Mylapore, Chennai. The original temple was lost under the rising sea. The pyramidal-shaped gopuram (temple top) is 121 feet high. In the carvings the Hindu goddess Parvati is shown as a peacock worshipping the Lord Shiva.

ABOVE Old Indian murals were painted with considerable skill by anonymous artists. Over the centuries some have been damaged, both by intent and decay.

LEFT: Just a short distance from Mumbai lies the Elephanta Caves of rock-cut temples dating back to the 5th century; the temples are dedicated to Shiva Mahadeva. Inside the complex is the Trimurthi Sadasiva, a huge sculpture 20 feet high representing Panchamukha Shiva, the five-headed Shiva, although only three of his heads are carved here—the other two are still encased in stone.

FAR LEFT: Standing on the southern bank of the river Tungabhadra in the village of Hampi is Vittala Temple. Inside the complex stands this stone chariot, or ratha, dedicated to Lord Garuda the huge mythical bird that transports Lord Vishnu. It is carved out of a single rock to resemble a temple chariot that traditionally carries temple idols out in procession; incredibly the stone wheels can still rotate. Work started on the temple in 1513 by Krishnadevaraya, and was continued by his successors Achuta and Sadasiva until 1565. The highly ornate main temple was built between the 15th and 17 centuries and is dedicated to Vishnu in the form of Vittala and stands in a rectangular enclosure 538 by 310 feet. The roof is supported by huge pillars, known as the Musical Pillars each of which carries a musical motif and is slightly different in height and width from its neighbor, making each pillar resonate differently to the music played in the courtyard.

ABOVE AND RIGHT: Hidden deep in a horseshoe-shaped ravine in dry hills of the Deccan in Maharashtra lies a remarkable complex of 28 elaborately carved caves. These were only discovered by the outside world in 1819 when a local scout pushed away dense vegetation to reveal the fantastic caves to some British soldiers. The caves had been elarorately carved by itinerant Buddhist monks and covered with intricate carvings and paintings. The earliest caves have been dated to the 2nd century B.C. and at its peak some 200 or so monks lived there, supported by a vast army of retainers, painters, and sculptors. Suddenly, in the 7th century, the complex was abandoned for unknown reasons and the site was soon almost completely forgotten.

LEFT AND ABOVE: The largest collection of prehistoric art in India is found in and around the caves at Bhimbetka in Madhya Pradesh and were only discovered as recently as 1958. The complex is made up of about 600 caves, some just overhanging rocks, where extraordinary paintings of wild animals decorate the walls. The prehistoric artists used twig brushes laced with animal fats and then dipped in a variety of pigments including charcoal, magnesium, colored soils, and various plant juices and extracts.

Hindu Empires and Islam c. 850 – 1560

Hindu Empires and Islam
c. 850 – 1560

The first great Hindu empire of this era was that of Chola, who rose to pre-eminence in around 850 after supplanting the Pallavas. By the reign of Raja Raja (985-1014) the empire covered the greater part of southern India and the Deccan plateau as well as incorporating overseas territories such as Sri Lanka, part of the Malayan peninsula, and Sumatra. Cholas' prosperity was due to its lucrative trading routes that stretched as far as North Africa, southern Europe, and Southeast Asia. The great wealth generated by this international commerce allowed the empire's rulers to undertake monumental building projects, especially at their own capital, Thanjavur, and Kanchipuram, that of the Pallavas, in what are now central and northern Tamil Nadu.

Frequent but periodic Islamic raids into the various kingdoms of northern India began in the early 1000s but the invaders' presence had became more permanent by the latter part of the century, by which time they controled vast tracts of land including Delhi and its environs, and Bengal. After beating off early attacks by the Mongols, the Muslim realm reached its greatest

PAGE 46-47: Ranthambore Fort sits 700 feet above the surrounding plain. Building started in 944 by the Chauhan Rajputs

RIGHT: The Tower of Victory in Chittaurgarh was built in 1440 by Maharana Kumbha to celebrate his victory over Mohamed Khiliji. About 157 narrow steps spiral up through nine stories to the terrace at the top of the tower. The tower is decorated with sculptures of Hindu deities.

FAR RIGHT: Kandariya Mahadeva temple in Madhya Pradesh was built c. 1050 at Khajuraho by the great Chandela king Vidyadhara. The main spire (shikhara) rises up 102 feet and represents Mount Meru, the holy mountain of Shiva and is surrounded by 84 miniature spires.

extent under Mohammed Tughlaq, who came to the throne in 1324. His vaulting ambition led him to make an unsuccessful and financially disastrous attempt to take over southern India that heralded the collapse of the empire. Thereafter the Islamic north split into several fractious splinter kingdoms that were unable to unite against later Mongol invasions. Ultimately, the Sultanate of Delhi fell to Tamerlane amid scenes of great slaughter in 1398.

The next great Hindu empire in the south emerged when various kingdoms banded together against the threat posed by the Muslim states to the north. The so-called Vijayanagar Empire became a power in 1336 and had its capital at Hampi in what is now central Karnataka. The empire's influence and power, which was founded on the control of the local trade in cotton and spices, spread over the following centuries, not least under the rule of Bukka I (c.1343–1379). Vijayanagar rule reached its peak in the 16th century by which stage the empire encompassed most of southern India and had a population of some 500,000 people.

The empires collapse was sudden and spectacular and came after the empire had been weakened by a succession of internal uprisings. Taking advantage of this unrest, the Vijayanagar capital was ruthlessly ransacked and looted by a confederation of the Muslim Deccan sultanates in 1565 after their crushing victory at the Battle of Talikota.

RIGHT: Tomb of Isa Khan Niyazi, an Afghan noble who served at the court of Sher Shah Sur. His tomb was built between 1547-1548 and is located in a walled garden enclosure near Delhi in the same complex that also contains Hunayun's Tomb (*see page 66*). It is octagonal in plan and is ringed by a deep verandah.

FAR RIGHT: Fort Golconda in Andhra Pradesh snakes for six miles across the top of a 400 foot high solid granite outcrop and was the capital of the seventh Qutb Shahi kings from 1518 until the late 16th century. Most of the fort was built in the 16th and 17 centuries although the oldest parts date from the early 13th century.

LEFT: In the Himalayan regions of northern India, Chinese and Tibetan styles of architecture predominated as this old ruined palace doorway shows.

FAR LEFT: Kunwar Math or Dulah Deo Temple at Khajuraho in Madhya Pradesh is the finest remaining temple of the original 85 temples built by the Rajputs, who ruled between the 9th and the 13th centuries. Much neglected for most a thousand years, only about thirty still remain. A unique feature of the Khajuraho temples is that, contrary to the norm, they are not enclosed within walls, but instead stand on a high terrace of solid masonry.

LEFT: The city of Bikaner in Rajasthan was originally founded in 1486 by Rao Bika (1465-1504) and rapidly grew larger. The architecture of Bikaner is particularly renowned for it intricate red sandstone window screens called *jharokas* which were carved in the near-by village of Dulmera. The screens allowed the women in purdah to watch the outside world while remaining hidden themselves.

FAR LEFT: The Quwwat-ul-Islam (The Might of Islam) was the first mosque to be built in India and stands in the shadow of the more famous Qutub Minar tower in Delhi. Although now ruined, it contains pieces looted from the 27 Hindu and Jain temples of Qila Rai Pithora, the city of the Rajput king Prithviraj Chauhan, giving it a unique combination of Indian and Islamic features with corbelled arches, floral motifs, Islamic calligraphy, and geometric patterning. The mosque was built between 1192 and 1195 by Qutub-ud-din Aibak, the first ruler of the Slave Dynasty, however various improvements were added by later generations.

LEFT: Inside the Musamman Burj, the beautiful large octagonal tower within the compund of Agra Fort. Mumtaz Mahal had lived here and it was here that Shah Jahan was imprisoned for seven years after being deposed by his son Aurangzeb. The Musamman Burj has a high open pavilion designed to catch the cool evening breezes drifting off the Yamuna River far below and views of the Taj Mahal in the near distance. According to legend, this is the last view enjoyed by Shah Jehan before he died.

FAR LEFT: Agra Fort in Uttar Pradesh was the great stronghold of the Moghul Empire and was built predominently from red sandstone between 1565 and 1571 by Akbar. The citadel ramparts run for almost a mile and a half high above a bend in the Yamuna River and contain within their bounds a number of important buildings. During his reign Shah Jahan converted part of the fort into a luxurious palace.

RIGHT: Our Lady of Immaculate Conception in Panjim, the capital of Goa. The first church here was probably built around 1541, but this was rebuilt in 1619. The great bell—reputed to be the second largest in the world—and known as the Bell of the Inquisition, came from the abandoned Church of St Augustine in 1871.

FAR RIGHT: An isolated monastery high up in the Himalayas. Some monasteries welcome trekkers and travelers but others are so isolated that it is very rare for outsiders to enter the holy buildings.

ABOVE: This old stupa in Ladakh looks as old as the Himalayas behind. Ladakh is high up in the mountains of northern India and is the remotest and most sparcely populated region. It is separated from China and Pakistan by the Himalaya and Karakoram ranges repectively.

RIGHT: Namgyal Tsemo Gompa (monastery) was built in 1430 by King Tashi Namgyal on top of Namgyal Tsemo peak overlooking the town of Leh in Ladakh. Inside the monastery is a three-story high, solid gold Maitrieya Buddha, also called the Laughing Buddha. Tashi Namgyal Fort further up the hill is ruined.

ABOVE AND RIGHT: Historically Ladakh was important for its strategic location at the trading crossroads between China, Tibet, and India. Many people here are of Tibetan descent, indeed, thanks to its remote mountain beauty and Buddhist culture, Lahakh is sometimes called "Little Tibet." In the 13th century during the advance of Islam across south east Asia, Ladakh looked to Tibet for religious guidance and support and in response Buddhism took a strong hold on the country. But by 1600 neighboring Muslim states imposed their influence and many locals converted to Islam.

The Early Mughals 1526 – 1605

The Early Mughals 1526 – 1605

The Mughal Empire was relatively short-lived, lasting a little less than 200 years, but at its height it covered most of the Indian sub-continent and its Muslim rulers were renowned for their patronage of the arts, and in particular architecture, and their general tolerance of other religions. The empire was founded by Babur (1483–1530)—a descendant of both Genghis Khan and Tamerlane—who invaded the Punjab from Kabul, his capital in Afghanistan, in 1525. His crushing victory over the numerically superior but technologically inferior forces of the Sultan of Delhi, Ibrahim Lodi, at the Battle of Panipat during the following year laid the foundations for the empire.

Babur's son and successor, Humayun (1508-1556), suffered a setback at the hands of the powerful ruler of eastern India, Sher Shah, in 1539 and was forced to withdraw into Iran. This reverse was only temporary. Sher Shah died in 1545 and Humayun returned the following year to reassert his authority. His dominance was confirmed in 1555 when he conquered Delhi. Humayun did not enjoy the fruits of victory for long as he died the following year and was succeeded by his young son, Akbar (1542-1605), whose momentous reign lasted 49 years. During this period he pushed the empire's borders outwards to cover a huge area and ensured that Mughal rule across India was unchallenged.

Akbar was only 13 at the time he became emperor but dismissed the regent, Bairam Khan, who ruled in his name four years later. The young emperor had first to successfully deal with various internal rebellions but was then able to embark on a succession of campaigns that greatly added to the extent of the empire. These began in 1561 and continued until 1600 by which time Akbar was undisputed master of all of northern India. He was, however, much more than a conqueror and his list of achievement ultimately earned him the title of Akbar the Great.

Akbar also embarked on various financial reforms, was very supportive of commerce and was also an ardent promoter of both the arts and science. Although born a Muslim, he was tolerant of the followers of other religions, not least towards the Portuguese Christian missionaries, although they failed to convert him. He also recognised that he had to reach an accommodation with the numerically superior Hindus who lived within his empire. Rather than view them as potential enemies, he made the most capable of them his advisers and administrators. Akbar was also a social reformer of note—slavery was abolished in 1582, *sati* (the practice of a widow being burned to death with her deceased husband) was banned, polygamy was for the large part ended, and widows were given the right to remarry.

PAGE 64-65: Meherangarh Fort sits 400 feet above the city of Jodhpur in Rajasthan and is one of the largest forts in India. Building work started in May 1459 on Bhaurcheeria, the mountain of birds, however, most of the extant fortification dates from the mid-17th century when it was greatly extended by Jaswant Singh.

RIGHT: The tomb in Delhi of the second Mughal emperor Humayan is one of the best examples of early Mughal architecture. The magnificent tomb was ordered by the emperor's widow, Hamida Banu Begum, and work started in 1562. It is built of red sandstone inlaid with fine marbles and topped with a double dome, the first of its kind in India. Humayan's Tomb is part of a garden complex that contains other tombs including the older tomb of Isa Khan (*see page 50*).

LEFT AND FAR LEFT: Charminar—Four Spires—is a huge monument in Hyderabad, the capital of the state of Andhra Pradesh. It was built in 1591 using granite and lime mortar in the Cazia style of architecture. The monument was the inspiration of Quli Qutb Shah to celebrate the end of the plague: according to legend he prayed at this spot for the disease to end, vowing to build a masjid on the spot. Each side of the monument measures 65½ feet and each of the four minarets has four storeys and rises to 160 feet. Inside each minaret there are 149 steps winding up to the upper floor gallery and each has 45 prayer spaces but also large open areas for Friday prayers. At ground level all four sides are pierced by a giant arch 36 feet wide, rising to 65½ feet at the highest point. Originally each of the arches led to four royal roads.

RIGHT: Seven miles north east of Jaipur in the midst of the wild Aravalli Hills lies Amber Fort, named after the goddess Amba Mata, who the local Mina tribe worshipped as Mother Earth. The complex was begun in the 11th century but was considerably improved and extended by Raja Man Singh I (1590–1614) who developed it as a pleasure palace. The palace sits high above Maota Lake which originally supplied the main water supply for the complex. Much of the fort is decorated with elaborate carvings and the pleasure chambers were built so that the precious fresh air from the surrounding hills is collected and then cooled over channels of perfumed water before being circulated around the rooms.

LEFT AND PAGES 74 AND 75: Views of the Amber Fort, the capital of Kachwahas. Although the fort dates to 1592 it was modified by successive rulers over the following 150 years until the capital was moved to Jaipur by Sawai Jai Singh II in 1733.

THESE PAGES: Views of the desterted royal city of Fatehpur Sikri in Uttar Pradesh which between 1571 until 1585 was the capital city of the Mughal empire until the lack of sufficient water for the increasing populations of the palaces and city forced the move to Agra, 26 miles away—a day's march—in 1600.

Fatehpur Sikri—the City of Victory—was founded by Jala-ud-Din Akbar, the third Mughal ruler of India, and built in honor of the Sufi saint Salim Chishti in 1571 to celebrate the much desired birth of his son and heir Prince Salim in August 1569. Prince Salim was later to become Emperor Jahangir. The complex of monuments and temples are predominently built out of the local red sandstone in a mixture of various regional architectural styles, although Gujarati and Bengali predominate; this was because craftsmen from the different regions worked on the project bringing with them their own vernacular styles. The complex includes the Jama Masjid, one of the largest mosques in India.

LEFT AND PAGES 80 AND 81: The Golden Temple in Amritsar, Punjab is the spiritual center for Sikhs and their most sacred shrine. The Hari Mandir—The Temple of God—the actual Golden Temple itself, sits in the middle of a rectangular sacred pool—known as the Sarovar. The temple is connected to the rest of the complex via the narrow Guru's Bridge. The temple was completed in 1601 and built by Guru Arjun (1581–1606) who also compiled the Adi Granth sacred scriptures. The temple has four entrances to show its openness: anyone is welcome to enter the temple regardless of religion or sex providing they do not indulge in cigarettes, drugs, alcohol, or meat while they are there. Before entering a person must first cover their head to show respect and wash their feet in a small pool nearby. The temple had to be substantially rebuilt in the 1760s after being badly damaged during an Afghan attack led by Ahmed Shah Abdali.

PAGE 80: The Golden Temple lit up at night by thousands of lights takes on a different aspect.

PAGE 81: A young Sikh gazes out from the Golden Temple.

The Later Mughals 1605 – 1707

The Later Mughals 1605 – 1707

Akbar the Great died in 1605 and was succeeded by Jehangir (1569-1627), who was able to defeat several challengers to his authority—in part thanks to the resoluteness of his wife, Nur Jahan—but he did not make any great efforts to extent the empire he inherited. Jehangir, who was a patron of the arts, died in 1627 while journeying to Kashmir and was succeeded by one of his sons, Shah Jahan (1592-1666), who moved quickly to consolidate his position by having all of his nearest male relatives and possible rivals executed. Despite his forces being defeated by Sikhs in the Punjab on two occasions and losing Kanadahar to the Persians in 1653, he was able to extend Mughal power in the Deccan. Shah Jahan was a notable sponsor of architectural projects and an able administer, but he suffered several years of illness before his death during which time his four sons vied for power.

The eventual victor was his third son, Aurangzeb (1618-1707), a narrow-minded autocrat who ruled an empire that was coming to an end thanks to

PAGE 82: India is a land of forts and seemingly impregnable bastions, although such imposing structures are constant reminders of past conflicts they are also magnificent pieces of military engineering.

RIGHT: The Jal Mahal Palace lies in the Nahargarth Hills of Rajasthan and dates back to 1799 when it was built in Rajput style as a pleasure palace for royal duck-shooting parties. Built by Sawai Pratap Singh this grand shooting lodge lies on the route beside the Amber Fort road from Jaipur and is surrounded by the manmade Man Sarobar lake. The building is joined to the lakeside by a causeway but the palace is now abandoned because the lower four floors are under water in the monsoon season, although in the hot summer the lake can disappear altogether.

both internal and external pressures. Some of the wounds were self-inflicted. Aurangzeb embarked on a policy of ambitious and unnecessary territorial expansion but this military effort was funded by increasingly burdensome and unpopular taxes. His decision to move the Mughal capital from Agra in what is now modern Uttar Pradesh to the self-styled Aurangabad in what is now central Maharashtra during 1653 was unpopular. His authority was further weakened by growing Hindu resentment at the high rate of taxation, a general return of religious intolerance, and the growing stagnation of the Mughal court and its administrators.

The empire also faced pressure from outside forces. The Marathas rose to prominence in central India inspired by the exploits of the anti-Muslim Hindu leader Shivaji during the period 1646 and 1680, but power eventually rested with hereditary government ministers. These initially supplied the Mughals with much-needed troops but they gradually began taking over the weakened empire's lands. Aurangzeb's rule ended in chaos. Aside from the pressure being exerted by the Marathas, he also faced challenges from his own rebellious sons and died a fugitive in Ahmadnagar.

The end of the Mughal Empire was effectively marked by the sacking of Delhi in 1739 by the Persian king Nadir Shah. There were other Mughal rulers until the uprising against the British in 1857 but these held a largely ceremonial and symbolic office. They were emperors stripped of any real power who ruled an empire that existed in name only.

RIGHT: Mughals saw gardens as high art and important elements in placing buildings into a landscape: the emphasis is on symmetry and includes such essential elements as pools, fountains, and canals.

FAR RIGHT: Indian temple deity decorated for a festival.

LEFT AND FAR LEFT: The Hawa Mahal or Palace of the Wind is part of the City Palace complex built in Jaipur by Maharaja Sawai Pratap Singh in 1799. It was designed by Lal Chand Usta and built out of red and pink sandstone; at the base are two courtyards above which on the eastern side are three stories only one room deep. The Hawa Mahal is part of the womens' quarters and is constructed so that the ladies of the court could watch goings-on in the street outside from behind the elegantly and elaborately carved facade without being seen. The frontage contains 953 small window niches for the intimate chambers, each of which has its own carved lattice grill and tiny balcony. The windows are cleverly designed to make the most of even the very slightest breeze during the hot dry summer weather. The upper levels are reached from the hidden courtyard behind and can only be reached by ramps.

LEFT: The Jantar Mantar at Jaipur is the second of five observatories built in west central India between 1727 and 1734 by Maharajah Jai Singh II. The observatory contains large scale, highly accurate astronomical instruments that are beautiful geometric forms as well.

FAR LEFT: The crematorium of the Kachhawaha rulers of Jaipur are at Gaitore, a little over 9 miles from Jaipur on the road to Amber. The cenotaphs are known as *chhatri* and are made from white marble and elaborately decorated with beautiful carvings and colorful and delicate paintings (the latter now long gone). The three most grandoise cenotaphs belong to Sawai Ram Singh, and Sawai Madho Singh, but the biggest and most spectacular belongs to Sawai Jai Singh II (1686–1743), the founder of Jaipur.

THESE PAGES: The Jantar Mantar is the amazing early 18th century observatory built in Jaipur by Raja Sawai Jai Singh II. The Raja was a considerable and enthusiastic astronomer and he sent his emissaries out far and wide to collect the very latest astronomical instruments from around the world before he started building his observatories, of which there are five. This is his second, largest, and most famous observatory, built between 1727 and 1733. Among many other amazing things the instruments can mark time to the accuracy of a second. The observatory attracted scholars and scientists from all over India and Europe who marveled at its precision and facilities.

93

ABOVE AND RIGHT: The City Palace over looks Pichola Lake in the heart of Udaipur and was built by Maharana Udau Singh of the Sisodia Rajput family in the 16th century then subsequently greatly extended to its present magnificence by following rulers. The palace is made out of granite and marble in a combination of European and Chinese architectural styles and sits in magnificent gardens.

LEFT AND PAGES 96 AND 97: Jag Niwas, also known as the Lake Palace, was started in Udaipur in 1754 by Maharana Jagat Singh II. The palace is built on Jag Niswas island that occupies almost four acres in the middle of Lake Pichola. Surrounded by courtyards and gardens fillled with fountains and flowers the palace is now a very plush and luxurious hotel.

RIGHT: Sultan Fateh Ali Tippu (1750–1799) started building his summer palace retreat in about 1790 on the site of the original citadel. It is based on the Daria Daulat Bagh in Srirangapattana. Sultan Tippu—also called the Tiger of Mysore—called it Rashk-e-Jannat meaning Envy of Heaven. Made mainly out of wood it is now very dilapidated.

LEFT: The Great Gateway to the Taj Mahal was built in 1648 and is made from red sandstone inscribed with passages from the Quran.

FAR LEFT AND PAGES 104–105: The Taj Mahal is widely acknowleged as an architectural masterpiece. It is built with dazzling white marble from a nearby quarry at Makrana, near Jodhpur and is studded with 28 different types of precious and semi precious stones: amethyst from Persia, agate from the Yemen, jasper from Punjab, lapis lazuli from Ceylon and Afghanistan, malachite from Russia, mother of pearl from the Indian Ocean, chrysolite from Egypt, crystal and jade from China, turquoise from Tibet, and diamonds from Golconda. The Taj Mahal is a mausoleum for Mumtaz Mahal (meaning "Chosen of the Palace"), the favorite and second wife of Shah Jahan. He was devastated by her death while giving birth to their 14th child in 1629 and locked himself away for a week, when he came out he had turned completely gray; the kingdom was ordered into mourning for two years. The tomb itself lies deep within the building in a basement vault, it is inscribed with the 99 names of Allah and elaborately decorated with semi-precious stones. Shah Jahan is buried in a tomb nearby.

The British in India 1612 – 1947

The British in India 1612 – 1947

Britain was neither the first nor the last European power to occupy India—Goa was occupied by the Portuguese from 1510 to 1961—but the former had the far greater impact on the sub-continent. They first arrived as traders in 1612 in the guise of the East India Company, a body that established various outposts and would ultimately control India's destiny for the next nearly 250 years. The British had trading rivals including both Demark and the Netherlands, but their bitterest opponents were the French, whose involvement in India did not ebb away until the 1750s. Over time the British gradually changed from traders to rulers through the use of brute force and skilful diplomacy that took every advantage of local rivalries and political weakness. India was largely under British control by the beginning of the 19th century.

RIGHT AND FAR RIGHT: The Chhatrapati Shivaji Maharaj Vastu Sangrahalaya in Mumbai was formerly the Prince of Wales Museum of Western India and built to commemorate the visit of the Prince of Wales (later George V) to Bombay in the early 20th century. Designed by George Wittet in Indo-Saracenic style, the prince laid the foundation stone in 1905 and remains here in statue form (right). The building was completed by 1914 but did not open to the public until 1923 as it served as a military hospital during World War I. The facing stone were quarried locally and the dome was modelled after the Gol Gumbaz in Bijapur.

PAGES 106–107: Darjeeling in the Shiwalik Hills of West Bengal was developed during the British Raj as a hill station—it sits at around 7,000 feet—for Britons to escape the oppressive dry summer heat of the lowlands and cities. Typically, wives and children would pass the hottest months here with their husbands and fathers joining them when possible. The temperate climate was ideal for growing tea and the nearby hills are covered with tea plantations, many started by the British in the 1800s for growing the prized Darjeeling tea.

British rule was based on two principles. India remained a patchwork of self-administrated mini-states ruled by various types of princes but a system of central government with an English-speaking civil service was also developed. The British also began to exploit the country's rich natural resources—especially tea and cotton but also coffee, coal, and minerals—and tied the vast lands together with an extensive railroad network. There was one main challenge to British authority in India during this period and it came in 1857. Variously known as the Indian Mutiny or the War of Independence, the uprising failed but it led to the demise of the East India Company and the imposition of direct rule by the British government.

Opposition to British rule grew steadily throughout the first half of the 20th century and coalesced around the Indian National Congress, a body founded in 1885. The political climate changed completely in 1919 when British troops opened fire on a crowd of civilians in Amritsar, causing around 1000 casualties. Previously apolitical Indians flocked to support congress and found inspiration in its new leader, Mohandras Ghandi, who advocated a policy of non-violent non-cooperation.

World War II was the turning point. Britain was greatly weakened by its exertions and a new breed of politicians appeared who were less thrilled with the concept of empire. They also saw that if they did not act quickly the growing rift between Muslims and Hindus might lead to unrest on an almost unimaginable scale. Violence between the two communities broke out in August 1946 and seemed destined to worsen forcing the British government to act. A new viceroy, Lord Louis Mountbatten, was appointed and he announced that India would become independent on August 15, 1947. It was also revealed that the sub-continent would be partitioned into Muslim-dominated West and East Pakistan and a Hindu-dominated India proper, in what turned out to be a futile effort to prevent more inter-communal bloodshed.

LEFT: A preserved Indian locomotive: India is one of the few countries where steam trains still operate. All the early locomotives would have been founded and assembled in Britain and then brought to India on board ship. The railroads expanded rapidly in India: in 1851 the first commercial train ran hauling construction material, then around two years later the first passenger train ran between Bombay and Thana and from then on the railroads blossomed. Backed and encouraged by the British government the railroads rapidly expanded across the sub continent. By 1880 there was a network of nine thousand miles of track and by 1895 the first locomotives were being built in India.

RIGHT: Winding and turning roads among the tea plantations. The tea plant—*Camellia sinensis*—is an evergreen shrub or small tree that is harvested every eight to 12 days or so for its fresh shoots. Because of this regular cropping the plants do not grow very high and always look very neat and tidy. Older leaves contain stronger flavors and make different qualities of tea. The plant is indigenous to south east Asia and was introduced to India by the British as an ideal crop for the higher, temperate mountain climate.

LEFT: The "Toy Train" belonging to the Darjeeling Himalayan Railway Co (DHR) on the Batasia Loop during its journey between Siliguri and Darjeeling. The railroad was built in 1881 and runs for 54½ miles between the plains of West Bengal and Darjeeling. Towards the end of the journey the train slowly ascends to 7,400 feet at Ghum (the second highest station in the world) and then descends 6,812 feet to Darjeeling. This is done through an elaborate series of five Z bends and three loops, the most famous of which is the Batasia Loop.

ABOVE: Presiding over transport in Mumbai (formerly Bombay) is the Chhatrapati Shivaji Terminus, originally known as Victoria Station, the furthest western terminus for Central Railways of India. Construction started on the building in 1878 to a Victoria Gothic Revival design by F.W.Stevens. The station was originally named after the queen empress on Jubilee Day, 1887 and opened to the public on January 1, 1882. The resulting building is a particularly fine early example of a unique school known as "Bombay Style" that appeared when British architects worked with Indian architects and craftsmen and combined their two very diverse architectural traditions.

INDIA

FAR LEFT: Ajmeri Gate in the old city of Jaipur, Rajasthan. Also known as the Pink City, Jaipur was founded in 1727 by Sawai Jai Singh who surrounded his new city with a great wall 20 feet high and nine feet wide. Ajmeri Gate lies to the south and is one of the four main gates to the city.

LEFT: The Delhi Gate was designed by Edwin Lutyens and built as a memorial to the 70,000 Indian soldiers who died during World War I, many of them on foreign fields and a long way from home. Work started on the red Bharatpur stone landmark in 1921 and the monument was completed and dedicated ten years later. An additional 13,516 names are engraved on the arch and foundations to form a separate memorial to the British and Indian soldiers killed in 1919 on the North-West Frontier during the Afghan War.

LEFT AND FAR LEFT: Jaswant Thada is a white marble memorial built in 1899 in the city of Jodhpur in memory of Maharaja Jaswant Singh II. Although one of many memorials on this traditional cremation ground it is the biggest and most beautiful. In the background dominating the surrounding plain is the magnificent old Mehrangarth Fort on top of its 400 foot escarpment. Some of its ramparts are cut from the rock itself and the fort can only be entered through a long zigzag pathway that runs through a series of fortified gateways.

LEFT: Is this in England? No, St Paul's Cathedral is in fact thousands of miles away in Kolkata, although clearly inspired by Norwich Cathedral. It was designed by William Nairn Forbes and completed after eight years in 1847. The tower was badly damaged by an earthquake in 1934, necessitating a rebuild.

RIGHT: Another favorite retreat for the British during the long hot Indian summers was the southern Indian town of Munnar in Kerala. At between 5,000 and 8,000 feet the rolling hills and equable climate were ideal for vast tea plantations. In addition the area grows various spices—pepper, cardamom, cinnamon, nutmeg, ginger, garlic, cloves, and vanilla.

Modern India 1947 to the Present

Modern India 1947 to the Present

The birth of an independent Indian state was painful in the extreme. There had been Hindu-Muslim violence before independence and its continued as what had been British India split into West and East Pakistan, both largely Muslim but with Hindu and Sikh minorities and India, largely Hindu but with its own Muslin and Sikh minorities. Vast numbers of ordinary people—at least 250,000—were slaughtered on both sides, especially in the Punjab, while ten million fled their homes to escape persecution. There were also issues over border demarcations, particularly in Kashmir, which quickly led to a brief war between India and Pakistan. There was a second war over Kashmir in 1965 and border clashes in 1971 when East Pakistan emerged as independent Bangladesh. Finally India and China clashed over a disputed border in 1962 and this issue, like that of Kashmir, remains unresolved and bitterly contested.

There have been various examples of inter-communal violence in India down to the present. This has largely been between Muslim and Hindu extremists but has also involved Sikh separatists seeking a homeland. Although many thousands of ordinary people have died at the hands of the extremists, India's elite has also suffered. Mohandras Ghandi fell victim to a Hindu radical in 1948, while Indira Ghandi was assassinated by her Sikh bodyguard in 1984

RIGHT: There are 52 bathing Ghats in the little town of Pushkar in eastern Rajasthan and 400 temples. The only temple in India dedicated to Brahma, the god of creation, is in Pushkar and the town is also one of the five *dhams* (pilgrimages) that Hindus aspire to make—the others are Badrinath, Puri, Rameswaram, and Dwarka. Otherwise the town is famous for its colorful annual camel fair every October–November—specifically for the full moon day of Kartnik.

after ordering Indian troops to evict Sikh radicals from the Amritsar temple. Her eldest son, Rajiv, was also a victim to violence, when he was killed by a supporter of a Sri Lankan separatist group in 1991.

Although the relationship with Pakistan overshadows all else, even more so now that both states have developed nuclear weapons, India remains plagued by other issues, not least the growing division between the vast number of poor and the tiny minority of rich. The country remains overwhelmingly rural— some 75 percent of people live outside the cities in the countryside but the latter seem likely to grow even more rapidly as India's burgeoning urban-based economy seeks a steady supply of cheap labor. Thus the eradication of poverty, an issue that has dogged India since Independence, remains the top domestic priority for politicians but other issues are rising up the agenda.

Aside from issues of creaking economic infrastructure, many of these relate to environmental threats. Something like 65 percent of India's agricultural land has been degraded by the overuse of chemicals since the 1960s but there are many other examples of over exploitation and greed—rampant deforestation, the excessive extraction of water, and growing air pollution among them. Unless these are addressed as a matter of urgency, it seems likely that the problems will only get worse as India becomes a fully developed nation.

RIGHT AND FAR RIGHT: Mohandas Karamchand Gandhi was the spiritual and political leader of India and the Indian independence movement. He is commemorated all over the country with memorials and statues. His opposition to British rule was personified by *Satyagraha*—the resistance to foreign tyranny through mass non-violent civil disobedience. By winning the respect and support of the world he eventually brought independance to India and earned himself the reverential title of Mahatma Gandhi, meaning "Great Soul."

LEFT: Varanasi (formerly Benares) stands on the bank of the River Ganga (Ganges) and is the most important and sacred pilgrimage destination for Hindus who come here in their thousands to worship at the shrine of Lord Kasi Viswanatha. Bathing in the Ganga is believed to wash away sins, and furthermore, rebirth is avoided by dying here in the holy city; meaning that believers are liberated from the cycle of life and death. Recently the historic practice of cremating corpses on the banks of the Ganga and then throwing the remains into the river has been banned in an attempt to reduce the water pollution.

FAR LEFT: India is a very religiously diverse country and most Indians practice a faith of one sort or another. The vast majority (over 80 percent) are Hindus, the vernacular religion, the next largest group are some 13 percent Muslims, then just over two percent are Christians, almost two percent Sikhs, then somewhat fewer Jains, Buddhists, Zoroastrians, and Jews.

ABOVE: The Vishwa Shanti Stupa—World Peace Stupa—at Vaishali, Bihar.

LEFT: Birla temple in Delhi was built in 1938 by Raja Baldev Birla and then inaugurated by Mahatma Gandhi. The temple is dedicated to the goddess Lakshmi although Durga and Shiva also share the temple with her, and Buddha has his own complex here as well.

LEFT: Pilgrims have made their way to Varanasi (formerly Benares) since time immemorial and consequently it has always been a place of great learning and importance and features prominently in many ancient Indian legends. Temples and shrines are found all over the city but especially beside the river Ganges. Thousands of pilgrims come to worship and perform an *abhishekam*—the ceremony of ablutions and symbolic offerings—with water taken from the Ganges. At the same time mantras are chanted to invoke blessings and inspire spirituality. Millions of pilgrims converge on Varanasi particularly at Shivaratri in the month of Aquarius for the biggest festival of the year.

PAGES 132–133: The state of Goa on the west coast of India was a Portuguese colony from the 15th century until 1962 and has long been a favorite laid-back holiday resort. The colony is famous for its decaying splendor and Indo-Portuguese architecture, but its principal attraction are the numerous splendid beaches bordering the Arabian Sea allied with the glorious climate.

LEFT: Vidhana Soudha in Bangalore is a huge granite building built between 1951 and 1956 in Neo-Dravidian style that also incorporates elements of Indo-Saracenic, Rajasthani Jharokha, and Dravidian styles. This imposing building is the seat of the state legislature of Karnataka and the largest legislative building in India. It was the idea of Shri Kengal Hanumanthaiah, chief minister of Mysore who traveled the world for architectural inspiration before embarking on the project. .

LEFT: Also known as the Blue City, Jodhpur is an unusually colorful place, even for India. Blue pigment is used on the walls of the houses to show that the building is the home of a follower of a Jodhpuri Brahmin, but the locals also believe that the color wards off mosquitoes. The practice makes Jodhpur uniquely vibrant.

LEFT: High up in the Himalayas isolated villages only have contact with the outside world through the intrepid trekkers who have sufficient strength and stamina to discover such unspoiled places.

FAR LEFT: The Bahá'í House of Worship, also known as the Lotus Temple, is surrounded by nine ponds and lies in the village of Bahapur near Delhi. It was designed in the form of a lotus flower by Fariborz Sahba and completed in 1986 and has won numerous architectural awards. People of all faiths are invited to worship here and millions of tourists visit the temple every year. The white marble building has nine sides made up of 27 free-standing "petals" arranged in clusters of three. Inside it can hold up to 2,500 people who access the temple through nine doors that open onto the central hall.

RIGHT: Large Jain Temple. The Jains are a small but influential dharmic religion and philosophy that has its roots in ancient India. Jains follow the teachings of Tirthankaras and have an ancient tradition of scholarship. The religion emphasises spiritual independence and equality of all life with particular emphasis on non-violence. There are many Jain *tirthas* (pilgrimage sites) right across India as befits this ancient, non-violent religion.

LEFT: Colored powder in an Indian market, such wonderful powders are liberally used in Hindu rituals, especially for Holi, the Festival of Colors. Holi marks the beginning of spring and takes place on the full moon of Purnima, at the end of March or early April. On the first day of Holi, bonfires are lit at night to signify the burning of Holika, a mythological Hindu demoness was was killed on Holi, so saving her brother Prahlad from their father King Hiranyakashipu. On the second day revelers throw colored powders, buckets of colored water, and water balloons at each other. Everyone ends up completely technicolor.

RIGHT: Kashmir has the reputation of being one of the most beautiful places on earth and one of the lovliest is Dal Lake where many of the locals live in *shikaras* or house boats. The summer capital and largest town in Kashmir is nearby Srinagar at 5,200 feet above sea level. Surrounded by snow-covered mountains the town lies on the banks of the Jhelum River and, east of the city, Dal Lake. The lake is made up of three distinct waterways, Gagri Bal, Lokut Dal, and Bod Dal, which are linked by a series of man-made causeways.

LEFT: A Buddhist shop. Buddhism is based on the teachings of Siddhartha Gautama, who became known as the Buddha. From its foundation in northern India it spread across the sub continent and then eastwards to China, Korea, and Japan. It flourished until the 13th century when many Buddhists changed religion. The religion remained strong in the Himalayan areas like Ladakh, Arunachal Pradesh, and Sikkim.

RIGHT: Library building for the Sri Siddhartha Institute of Technology (SSIT) in Tumkar, near Bangalore was completed in January 2004. Made up from dark green and gray-colored triangular laminated glass it is 102 feet in diameter and 77½ feet high.

LEFT AND FAR LEFT: Nandi is the Hindu bull god that the Lord Shiva rides, he is also the gatekeeper of the Shiva and every worshipper has to get the blessings of Nandi before proceeding to worship Lord Siva. A statue of Nandi faces the main shrine at every Shiva temple.

RIGHT: A fruit juice stall in Mumbai. Fresh fruit makes a very welcome and refreshing drink in such a hot and dusty city.

FAR RIGHT: Hindu cows being transported on a truck, normally they are allowed to wander freely as they please. Brahmin cows or Zebu are associated with the god Shiva and are native to India. They are usually gray or white, have a large shoulder hump, long dangling ears, and a heavy dewlap.

RIGHT: Saat Rasta is Mumbai's most famous dhobi ghat or "washing place" and is the outdoor laundry area near Mahalaxmi train station. This family business is handed down from one generation to the next. Traditional laundrymen collect the dirty laundry, and for a very small charge, take it to one of the ghats or outdoor laundries. There among the rows of concrete wash pens, the clothes are soaked in soapy water, thrashed on a flogging stone, then tossed into huge vats of boiling starch and hung out to dry. When ready they are ironed and neatly folded and then taken back to their owners. At Saat Rasta almost two hundred dhobis and their families work together.

LEFT: The Gandhi Mandapam at Kanyakumari in Tamil Nadu was built on the spot where the urn containing the ashes of Mahatma Gandhi was kept for public view before a portion of its contents were immersed in three seas—the Arabian Sea, the Indian Ocean, and the Bay of Bengal. The building resembles an Orissan temple and was designed so that at midday on Gandhi's birthday (October 2), the sun's rays fall on the place where his ashes were kept.

BELOW: The Vivekananda memorial at Kanyakumari was built in 1970 to commemorate the visit of Swami Vivekananda in 1892.

LEFT: The rich waters around Kerala provide a living for many local fishermen, but the work is a hard and competitive and fishing is not a well paid occupation. There are some 2½ million fishermen in Kerala who provide around 20 percent of India's fish production. In 2006 there were an estimated 28,000 country boats, 27,000 mechanised boats, and 5,000 trawlers working out of Kerala. Much of the fish is sold at early morning beach markets.

LEFT: In Kerala even the trucks (or lorries as they are more often called here) are brightly decorated. There is great competition between the owners to have the best decorated machine and there are specialist places offering truck painting.

ABOVE: Despite the Indian economy being at the cutting edge of technology there is still a place for a slower, less modern way to earn a living, as this man delivering Kerosene shows.

Photo Credits

Map page 9 courtesy Mark
Franklin.
All photographs **Shutterstock
via Jo St Mart** unless specified:
2, 6, 18, 22, 60–61, 141 Chloe
Hall; 4, 86, 116 Wendy Connett;
10, 12, 17, 72, 74–75, 78, 81, 94,
95, 96, 98 Lisa Young; 49 Fuste
Raga; 50 Walter Bibikow; 53
Bjorn Svensson; 57 wikipedia;
80 Yadid Levy; 91 Jtb Photo; 92
Sybil Sassoon; 118 P. Narayan.

Corbis: 46-47 Martin Harvey/
fotolibra: 64-65 Alan Ward;
122, 150, 153, 156, 156-57
(both) Peter Herbert; 151, 152,
154-55 Ron Boon